The Carpenter's Tools

A  DRAMA RESOURCE

THE CARPENTER'S TOOLS

12 Contemporary Monologues on the Disciples

by
Jerry Cohagan

 PUBLISHING COMPANY

KANSAS CITY, MO 64141

CONTENTS

ACKNOWLEDGMENTS

Several authors' works have aided me immensely in the writing of these monologues. I have relied most heavily on Emil G. Kraeling's fine work *The Disciples* for historical and legendary background information on the apostles. I also wish to thank Mr. Frederick Buechner for his imaginative book *Peculiar Treasures: A Biblical Who's Who.* And I would be remiss not to mention the creative spirit of Mr. Clarence Jordan and his fervent writings in *The Cotton Patch Version of Luke and Acts* and *The Cotton Patch Version of Matthew and John.*

Finally, and most importantly, I wish to thank my wife, Lynda, for her willingness to listen, suggest, and above all else, encourage.

INTRODUCTION

When Christ gathered the beginnings of His church around Him, He could not have chosen a more diverse lot: a tax collector, some fishermen, a scribe of the Jewish law, a cousin, a writer, a revolutionary, a skeptic, and even a traitor. They seem an extraordinary lot when we attach names such as St. Peter and St. John to them. But in our perspective of 2,000 years, we often forget that their friends, and especially Christ himself, knew them as we know our friends and neighbors, as Pete and Johnny, maybe even Jack.

It was a desire to know those 12 very ordinary fellows as if they were my best friends that brought this book about. What would the apostles be doing if they lived in my day? Where would they work? Who would they "hang out" with?

And so began this project of transporting those 12 guys 2,000 years forward to my day and age. Not only did I discover 12 new friends, but I discovered that the Christ who took that ragtag bunch of fellows and transformed them into the foundation of His church is still doing it. He's doing it with me and my neighbors; His redemption is continually reaching down and transforming some very ordinary people into His tools.

I hope these monologues will enhance your worship, whether used in conjunction with a sermon, special music, or an evening of drama. May these voices sound familiar and may they remind us of a Savior who builds His kingdom on the likes of you and me.

To
Chase

My prayer
is that you would
be a tool for the Carpenter

PETER

NOTE: Peter is by far the most mentioned disciple in the Gospels. He seems to be involved firsthand in more stories and miracles of Jesus than any of the others. Peter never hesitated to give Jesus a piece of his mind, even when he really couldn't afford to spare it. Peter never weighed the pros and cons of his actions; he just acted. He never thought about what was politically correct; he just dove in—even if he couldn't swim.

Fortunately, Jesus Christ continually corrected, rescued, and loved Peter. How such an obscure fisherman came to represent Christ's church is indicative of how Christ claims each of us for His very own—no matter our worth or value in the eyes of the world. Whether Peter was a great man or whether greatness was thrust upon him matters little. What matters is that Peter was driven by his love for Jesus. It consumed him. To serve Christ was his passion. And Jesus will always honor such a heart. For Jesus is always faithful, even when we are not.

(AT RISE: Peter is wearing work slacks or jeans and a T-shirt with "Don't Mess with Texas" imprinted on it, if available. He has a well-worn straw cowboy hat on as well. He is squatting down on his haunches working a large commercial fishing net through his hands, checking it for holes and tears. He has a strong, muscular build and is in his 30s.)

PETER *(speaking with a slight Texas drawl, not overdone, almost to himself):* His last words to me were, "You're young now, and you go wherever you want to. But when you're old you'll stretch out your hands just like I did, and folks'll lead you where you don't want to go . . . so follow Me." *(Shakes his head in mild confusion, then looks up and addresses the audience)* He said that to me after I'd already muddled it up again. He said it to me right here on the beach, after the fact that He'd already stretched out His hands and died. *(Looking at his palm)* My hands are still pretty rough. A lot of scars and calluses from haulin' the nets. His hands were pretty rough too, though, the first time I shook 'em. He worked the wood for some 30 years with His daddy. Just about as long as I been doin' this.

(Letting the net fall, stands up, boisterous) You see, I'm a Texas boy, born and bred. That means two things: We're loud and we're proud. We ain't necessarily known for bein' smart as much as for bein' loyal. I been a shrimper here off the coast of Galveston my whole life, just like my daddy was and my daddy's daddy before

that. I know these waters here in the Gulf better than I know the land. It's all I've ever done, and I expected that it was all I'd ever do . . . and that it'd be enough. *(Beat, then)* But it ain't no more.

I dropped the nets for good right after I'd hauled in the biggest catch we'd ever had, thanks to Jesus. Anybody who knew the currents that good was good enough for me. I shook His hand and said, "You're my man." He slapped me on the back and said, "And you're Mine." And that's when the trouble began. Seems I just couldn't ever quite get it right.

Take for instance the time we boys were all out on my boat here in Galveston Bay. Our lives had all been changed since we'd took up with Jesus—the miracles, the healings, and the crowds. Anyway, we'd left Him on the beach and we were all trying to get on up to Baytown to get away from the crowd, but we'd been buckin' a strong headwind and thunderstorm most the night. Well, suddenly we see this yellow spirit floatin' across the waves movin' toward us! We were all ready to jump ship when this ghost turns out to be Jesus in a rain slicker, and He starts laughing and yellin', "Hey, you bunch of scaredy cats! How 'bout showin' a little courage? I ain't even wearing my rubbers, y'all!" Well, He'd pretty much given us all a heart attack. And I'd never been one to mince words, so I let Him know it!

(Angry) "You think that's funny, Jesus! We got a group pulse rate here higher than these squalls! You think You're so high and mighty, I outta walk right out there and get Ya!"

Well, Jesus just stops right where He is and smiles. *(Slight tone of egging him on)* "Come on, Pete."

(Looks around rather begrudgingly) Well, I'd done it again. Engaged my mouth before my brain. What was I gonna do? The other guys were all looking at me, waiting to see whether I'd put my money where my mouth was. So I kept my eyes locked on Him and hit the water runnin'. I don't know if it was courage or stupidity! But I was doin' it! There I was—wind surfin' without a board! Then about halfway out, a strange thought occurred to me. *(Stupidly)* "I cain't swim. I never could! I ain't even wearin' a life jacket! I cain't do this!"

And sure enough, by now I'm up to my neck in it screamin', "My God, save me!"

And, of course, He did. And while He's wrappin' blankets around me and my teeth are chatterin' He says *(mock surprise, teasingly)*, "Why, Pete, you're all wet. Why such little faith?"

(Angrily through chattering teeth) "'Cause I can swim 'bout as good as a rock can float!"

Well, Jesus grins and then takes off His slicker and the storm immediately stops and it gets real quiet all of the sudden. It was eerie the way He just glanced up at the sky and made it get so still and calm. It was like He wanted to be sure I didn't miss any of the words He spoke to me. He looked down at me there, shiverin' on the deck, and says *(intensely)*, "Don't think about what you *can't* do. Think about what you *can* do. Never doubt me, Pete. I'll always be there."

(After a moment) Well, like I said, I may not be much for smarts, but I'm bloodhound loyal. And the incident did change my attitude toward the man a bit. After that I swallowed my pride and even ate my own words. *(With a sense of awe)* See, I began to realize that He *was* high and almighty.

He even so much as asked us once who we thought He was. Well, several of the boys kinda hemmed and hawed around and said that folks were callin' Him a prophet, a psychic, even a madman. But that isn't what He asked. He was askin' us who *we* thought He was. He was wantin' us to stand up and be counted. I looked around at the boys and nobody seemed willin' to voice what we all knew and feared. Ever'body was kinda clearin' his throat and glancin' around, lookin' ever'where but at Him. Johnny was starin' at his hat like he'd never really seen it before; Matt was busy diggin' under his fingernails, searchin' for gold I guess. Jimmy was starin' down at his boots, scuffing the dirt about. And Judd was jinglin' the change in his pocket, a habit whenever he got nervous. Well, I couldn't believe it. We were all a bunch of lily-livered chickens. But I knew it was time to put up or shut up, and I never been one to fear the sound of my own voice. So I rose up and looked Jesus in the eye *(reverently)*, "You're the Christ, the Son of the living God."

Jesus looks real proud at me and says, "God bless ya, Pete! There ain't no way you coulda come up with that on your own. Ya got holy insight! You're the rock I'll build My church on."

(Sticking his chest out proudly) Well, if a rooster ever had an opportunity to crow that was it. Then Jesus starts in about headin' on down to Corpus Christi and dyin' . . . some crazy plan of His. Since I'd just been told I had holy insight, I pulled Him aside and thought I'd share some more. "Jesus, stop all this foolishness," I said. "You ain't never gonna die!"

Before I had a chance to take a breath, He turned and said, "Get away from Me, Satan! Now you're talkin' like a rock in My way, a boulder to crack My shins on. You're thinkin' for yourself again, and that always gets you in trouble."

(Exasperated) I'd say one thing and He'd call it divine inspiration, and then I'd proceed to say another and He'd call me the devil! Well, I got skin thick as an armadillo, but I don't need to tell ya that purty much took the wind outta my sails. So I shut up . . . but not for long.

A few weeks later we was all holed up in Corpus settin' down to supper. Jesus starts breakin' the biscuits and passin' the cup like always when He says, "I want ya'll to know that this bread is My busted body. And this wine is My blood. As often as ya'll eat and drink, I pray you'll think of Me and what I'm about to do for ya."

Well that purty much curbed our appetite a bit. And right away Judd starts jinglin' his change in his pocket again. And all us boys could see Jesus' heart was real heavy. I might be thickheaded, but I knew enough to know what Corpus Christi meant. So I raised up again and said *(demonstratively)*, "No, Lord. This ain't gonna happen to You! There ain't no way this is gonna be our last supper."

Without even lookin' up at me He says, "Peter, I wish it weren't so. But before the sun rises over the Gulf, you're gonna disown Me . . . not once, but three times."

(Adamantly) "Never, my God! I'll die for You!"

Slowly He lifted His head and locked His eyes on me. *(Achingly)* "Aw, Pete. Your words are truer than you know. Lucifer wants to pour you like water through a fishin' net. But I been prayin' for ya, Pete. That your faith will hold, even when your actions fail. And after you make your way back to Me, I want you to be strong for the boys."

(Stunned, slowly) His words cut me to the bone. And at that moment, all I know was that my chest was so tight it was all I could do to breathe in that dead silence.

(Beat, then) When the Rangers came to take Him away we all ran like jackrabbits. None of us stood by Him. I hung around by His cell until the jailer asked me if I knew the prisoner. "I'm not sure," I said. "No . . . no, I don't think I do."

It got easier after that. On my way outside I bumped into the deputy sheriff who asked me what I was doin' there.

"Nothin' . . . I thought I knew somebody here. But I don't."

(Building in intensity) By now I was runnin' toward the bay when somebody behind me yelled, "Hey, Pete! They got your God all locked up!"

And I raised my fists and shouted across the whole Gulf of Mexico *(screaming with his eyes closed)*, "I don't know Him!"

And I opened my eyes to see the sun write my denial across the sky in blazin' scarlet. *(Breaking down)* And with it my chest burst open, leavin' nothin' but a gaping hole where my heart used to be. You see, I always thought I knew my own heart . . . that I was a man of action. But when it came right down to it, I had feet of clay. *(Defeated)* I knew I was done for. All my hope had died with Him.

(Kneels down on his haunches and picks up the net) So I went back

to the only thing I knew. And I spent my days throwing out my nets, knowin' I'd never catch what I'd lost. And then one evening, just before sunset, I heard a voice callin' from the shore."Hey there, you bunch of scaredy cats! How 'bout showin' some courage?"

(Laughing joyously) I leaped overboard! I don't know if I swam, waded, or walked on water, but I got to Him and fell into His arms!

He threw back His head and laughed, "Why, Pete! You're all wet again! Come on. I got a fish fry goin' on up the beach for you and the boys."

(To the audience) You see! I was *finally* right about somethin'. Corpus Christi wasn't our last meal together. But somehow I knew this one was. After we ate our fill, Jesus took me aside and we walked along the shore. "Pete, I gotta know somethin'. Do you love Me?"

I said, "I never meant to turn my back on You, I just—"

"Pete, I gotta know. *(Gently)* Do you love Me?"

"I'm just a stupid fisherman, Lord. I got a big mouth and sometimes it gets me into trouble—"

(Interrupting again, insistent but gentle) "Pete, I gotta know. Do you love Me?"

(Beat, then softly) And my heart was broken. *(Full of emotion)* "Oh, Jesus. You know that I do." And I wrapped my arms around Him and clung to Him like the drownin' man I was.

After a moment, He raised me up. *(Gently)* "Peter, I love you too. *(Joyously)* And I want you to have a love for Me as big as all of Texas! Don't you see? We got bigger fish to fry now. You're strong as a rock and young now, and you go wherever you want to. But when you're old you'll stretch out your hands just like I did, and folks'll lead you where you don't want to go . . . so follow Me."

And at that moment, I understood. And for once in my life I didn't speak out of turn. I realized that even though I failed Him time and again, I was redeemed. And it finally sunk in that He is always faithful, even when I ain't.

(With a little bit of his bravado back, proudly) And I would count it an honor to die for my God. *(Smiles and gestures expansively)* Because, you see . . . I got a heart for Jesus as big as all of Texas!

(Beat, then notices his palms) My hands are still rough, and I imagine I'll always have the smell of fish under my nails. But that's OK. *(Tosses down the net and looks at audience)* I do good to remember what I been delivered from . . . *(Blackout)*

ANDREW

NOTE: The scriptural basis for this monologue is found in John 1:19-41. Besides Andrew being the first disciple of Jesus, John suggests several interesting things: Andrew is the first of the 12 disciples to recognize that Jesus is the Messiah; it is Andrew who brings his more famous brother, Simon Peter, to meet Jesus Christ; and in so doing, he is noted as winning the first recruit of the new faith. And by leading his brother to Christ, Andrew may well have done more for the church and the cause of Jesus than any of the other disciples.

(AT RISE: Andrew enters carrying several fishing poles, a tackle box, and net. He is wearing hiking boots, a flannel shirt, and jeans. He also has on a backpack that appears full. There is a sleeping bag tied on top of it as well. He has a couple days' growth of beard and is in his late 20s to early 30s. He appears very excited about something as he rushes around looking for his brother.)

ANDREW *(yelling as he rushes on from stage right):* Hey, little brother! Where are you? I got big news! We've been waiting our whole lives for this! *(Shrugs off backpack and drops poles and equipment)* Come on, now! *(Rushes upstage left, yelling)* No kiddin' around. Where are you? *(Muttering under his breath, crosses downstage right, looking)* This is just like him, says one thing and does another. *(Yelling again)* I gotta talk to you! Now! I mean it!

    (Turns and notices his imaginary brother entering stage left, immediately crosses and begins to mime pulling him downstage center) Oh, there you are! Where've you been? You're late. We were supposed to meet here by four o'clock. *(Listening for a moment)* Well, I know that was yesterday, but— *(As if he's being interrupted)* Yeah, I know I'm a day late—I know I didn't show up—yeah, I'm sure you were worried, I—I know that, if you'll just calm—you don't have to yell, I can hear you just fine—if you'll just stop yelling, I can explain. *(Finally yells back)* You're my brother, not my mother! Calm down and I'll tell you what happened. Boy, that temper is gonna do you in one o' these days.

    Now, are you ready to listen to me? *(Getting really tickled with excitement, begins pacing)* 'Cause you are not gonna believe what happened to me! You ready? You sure? *(Motions for him to sit downstage center)* You better sit down. *(Stares up at him, slightly higher than eye level)* I mean it, brother. You really ought to sit down for this. *(Stares at him, follows him down as imaginary brother finally sits)* Good. *(Unable to contain his glee, almost childlike)* This is so exciting! *(Faces downstage, as if talking right at him)* You ready for this? *(Takes a deep breath then slowly, with emphasis)* I have met . . . the Messiah!

(His eyes jump up, as if his brother has leapt to his feet and is yelling at him again) Yeah, I know— *(As if agreeing with everything his brother is yelling at him)* That's what I thought too—been in the woods too long—ate some bad mushrooms—talking to the trees— *(Begins backing up as if his brother is in his face, defensive)* Hey, don't point that finger in my face. You may be bigger, but I can still take you! *(Beat, then on second thought)* Maybe . . . if I have to. Just don't make me prove it! *(Puts his hands up, placating his brother)* Just let me tell you the whole story. Then you can decide whether to zip me up in my mummy bag and haul me down off the mountain or to go meet the man for yourself, OK?

Well, as you know, I was guiding these men, the Levite party, on back into the Wind River Range to do some serious trout fishing. Come to find out, these boys were all from the East Coast. They were all a bunch of religious professors and theologians from some highbrow seminary back in Boston, I guess. *(Chuckling)* Boy, talk about your fish outta water. One guy actually had a waffle iron in his backpack. I guess when I told them the currents were strong up here, he thought I meant electrical. Well, anyway, I pitched camp for 'em and got 'em all squared away and said I'd be back in a few days to lead 'em out.

About the time I was ready to start back we all heard some crazy howling and moaning coming from up the north fork of the Green River. They all grabbed onto one another and began whispering, "What was that?" One guy said it must be a coyote, another proclaimed a wolf, and someone else said it was the wind whistling through the evergreens. I told 'em they were all wrong.

(Beat, then affectionately) Yeah, that's right. It was ol' crazy John howling away, wearing nothing but them camel hair hip-waders out in the middle of that freezing river, puttin' anybody under who'd pause long enough to listen to him proclaim the coming of the Lord. I told them John'd been roaming these woods for as long as we'd been running this fishing lodge . . . just living off of granola and tree bark, as far as we could tell. This didn't seem to sit too well with these boys.

They asked me, "By what right does he baptize people and proclaim the coming of God?"

I said, "Why don't you go ask him for yourselves." So they did.

But they couldn't even agree on who he was. One said he was Christ, another said he was Elijah, another said a prophet.

Ol' John yelled at 'em, "You're missing the point, folks! It's not who I am but who comes after me that matters. And you better beat a straight path toward Him through these trees when He comes! Because I ain't worthy to unlace His Rockports."

Well, that shut 'em up for a while and then he tied their brains in a knot with one o' his rambling riddles. And I quote *(rattling this off quickly)*, "The Man I'm talkin' about who comes behind me is really before me because He has surpassed me and that's because He is greater because He has exceeded me because He was before me. And I'll become lesser as He becomes greater. And that's the way it should be! Understand?"

Well, theologically speaking, that gave 'em all something to chew on as they scratched their heads, shrugged their shoulders, and made their way on back to camp.

But I decided I'd spend the night with ol' John and hear what else he had to say. *(Confidingly)* I know he seems kinda demented at times, but I can't help but be attracted to his words. *(Unable to quite express it, almost mysteriously)* There's a power wrapped up in his madness.

(Drawing his brother in, intensely) You and I've talked about it . . . how great it would be if maybe John was right. About someone coming to redeem us. Someone who could set us free from ourselves, one who would give our lives meaning. *(Almost in a hushed voice)* You know, a savior . . . *(Beat, then softly)* That's why I let him dunk me in the river, brother. Because I chose to believe in his words.

(Beat, then begins picking up his energy again, pacing about) Anyway, yesterday morning John and I were sitting on the banks of the river when I noticed this man hiking alone through the brush on the other side. Well, John just stands straight up and points. And for the first time in his life, for as long as I've known him, he says something straightforward *(in a hushed voice, with a sense of awe and reverence)*, "Look, the Lamb of God! Come to wash away the sins of man."

Well, you know me. I'm not like you. I tend to think things through a bit. But for some reason I didn't even hesitate. I just impulsively stood up, said, "See ya, John," and just started wading across the river to get to this man. I got about halfway out, where the current's really strong and was about to turn back, when this man yelled to me, "What is it you want?"

I yelled back, "I want to know where You're going!"

He paused a moment and then smiled and called to me, "Come on and you'll see!"

So I followed Him and spent the day with Him. And that's why I wasn't here yesterday.

(With conviction, sits on his haunches next to brother) Do you un-

derstand what I'm telling you? This is the One we've waited our whole lives for! This is the One ol' John's been raving about for years! I hiked on back here to the lodge as quickly as I could to find you. I'm tellin' ya, I got blisters on my blisters! *(Laughs, then seriously)* But I had to tell you first; nobody else knows yet.

(Stands to leave) So, come on, what are we waiting for? Let's go! *(Starts off stage right, as if to leave, then stops)* What? I know I'm not acting normal; I know it's not rational. *(Chuckling good-naturedly)* But why should you care? You're the one that's usually blown by every wind, so passionate and fiery in what you feel at the moment. *(Steps toward his brother, fervently)* But for this one time, it's me . . . I've taken that leap and put my faith in something I don't fully understand. *(Full of passion)* All I know is that this man is our Messiah. He is the Christ. *(With a sense of urgency)* And you gotta meet Him!

(Starts to exit, but brother obviously is hesitating, crosses to center and mimes resting his hands on his brother's shoulders, looking straight into his eyes) Listen to me, brother. I don't know what He has planned for us, but I think we're talking a major career change here. If we do this, I don't think anything is ever gonna be the same again. *(Smiles in wonder, then starts off again and stops)*

No, forget about the fishing lodge! The Zebedee brothers can run it for a while. *(Gets a couple steps further, turns again)* Don't worry about it! The Levite party can find their own way out.

(Starts off again, eager to be going, stops and sighs, exasperated) Listen to me, little brother. For once in your life don't be so bullheaded. Don't you get it? Nothing else matters but that we follow Him! *(Beat, then)* So come on, put the pole down and let's go. *(Smiles and mimes putting his arm around his brother, they begin to leave together, good-naturedly ribbing him)* I tell ya, Pete, you can be so hardheaded. Sometimes I think you're as dense as a rock. *(He exits hurriedly stage right, laughing.)*

JAMES

(AT RISE: James is standing by a table that is stacked with a bunch of Styrofoam containers holding carryout food. Behind the table is a cardboard box. He is an average-looking guy, dressed casually. He is any age over 20 and speaks with a slight southern drawl.)

JAMES *(counting the containers on the table, checking everything):* Let's see . . . 12 catfish plates, each with a side of beans, a side of coleslaw, two hush puppies, and a dozen large iced teas. *(An afterthought, yells offstage)* Oh! Can I get extra tarter sauce and some lemon wedges for the tea? *(Beat, then smiles at the imaginary waiter offstage)* Thanks, Pa.

(To the audience, delighted with himself) I love to do that to him. Johnny and I still show up here once in a while for supper. Pa's got the best catfish place in town, always has. It still steams him a bit that we walked out on the family business. But I think deep in his heart he understands. You see, he still gives us a 10 percent discount.

(Gets the cardboard box and starts putting the order in the box) Johnny and I used to work here. This is kind of a mom and pop shop, you could say. Pa's run the place ever since I can remember. But Ma came up with the name. *(With fanfare)* The Zippity Catfish Diner! *(Explaining quickly)* Zippity because Pa's name is Zeb and Ma's name is Dee. Zeb and Dee . . . get it? Zip-a-dee Catfish Diner!

(Shrugging his shoulders) Anyway, we almost did Pop in when we walked out. You see, it all happened so fast. Not a lot happens real fast down here, but this sure did. 'Bout five o'clock, just before the supper crowd starts showin' up, Pete and his brother Andy sashayed in to tell us they'd no longer be supplyin' us with their

catfish. They ran a catfish farm just outside Tupelo, and they were our number one suppliers. Told us they were hitchin' their futures to this travelin' salesman who was passin' through.

Well, Johnny and I were ready to bust their chops right then and there! And we might've if it hadn't been for this travelin' salesman showin' up right then. See, Johnny and I always seemed to be competin' with those boys. Anything we did, they'd done the day before. We always seemed one step behind them, especially Pete. But we knew, in a fair fight, we could take 'em.

And like I say, we was just preparin' to clean their plows when in walks their newfound hope. This guy walks in, picks up a carryout menu, and orders a mess of catfish with all the fixin's to go. When I asked Him if He was feedin' an army He said yes, He was, and that we were His newest recruits. We asked Him what bill of goods He was sellin'. He said that He wasn't *sellin'* anything. In fact, He said that He'd come to settle up an outstanding bill that we could never pay. *(Scratching his head)* What'd He mean by that?

Maybe it was His charisma and charm, and the fact that, besides Andy and Pete, we were the first ones He called. Or maybe it was the fact that we couldn't let Andy and Pete be one up on us. Whatever it was, we hung up our aprons and followed too. We ain't looked back since. There're only about a dozen of us who ain't glanced over our shoulder.

It seemed to Johnny and me that Pete was always hornin' in. So we tried to muscle him out whenever we could. We knew the man had taken a shinin' to Pete. But we'd also watched him put Pete in his place a couple times too. See, Pete could put his whole leg—right up to his kneecap—in his mouth if ya let him jabber long enough. But we knew we were still in the runnin' when Jesus let Johnny and me, along with Pete, go with Him alone a couple times.

The first time was when the local pastor of the Nondenominational Intermingling Apostolic Independent Hope Church of the Free Spirit sought Jesus out to tell Him his daughter was sick. Before the reverend could even get to Him, some of his flock caught up with him and told him it was too late, his little girl was already dead. Jesus told him not to listen to them but to just believe. And then He singles me, John, and Pete out to go on with Him up to the reverend's house. The other nine fellas all stood there moping around, sulking and pouting while I swaggered a bit as I walked away with the Master.

We get to the parsonage and the whole congregation is wailin' and gnashin' their teeth and carryin' on! Jesus yells to ever'body, "Stop all this commotion! Quiet down out here! Don't you know there's a little girl trying to sleep inside." Well, that set ever'body off again. We all knew she'd passed on. Some even laughed in His face. And I gotta admit that even Pete and John and me caught each other's eye and sniggered a bit. We began to wonder if maybe Jesus was off His nut. I mean dead is dead, ain't it?

And that's when Jesus pulls the three of us inside the house with Him and yanks us by the collar to the foot of the little girl's bed. He goes around to the side and picks up her hand and gently strokes it a couple times and says, "Come on, honey. It's time to get up." *(Dumbfounded)* And she did! And Jesus just looks at us standin' there like the Three Stooges with our mouths danglin' open. He says to us, "Give her something to eat and close your mouths. Maybe that'll keep your feet out of 'em for a bit."

I know the other guys thought maybe Jesus favored us three. But I began to wonder if maybe the only reason He took us with Him was because the other nine fellas believed Him and didn't need to be taught a lesson. I don't know . . . somethin' to think about.

You'd think I'da stopped swaggerin' by then. But I didn't. You see, Jesus' fame was still on the rise around here, what with all the healin's and such. In fact, a couple days ago He told us we were movin' on down the road toward Jackson. *(Eager)* I'm thinkin', "Jackson? That's the capital! There's no tellin' how big He's gonna be down there!"

Listen, before I tell ya what John and I did, I want ya to try and see it a bit from our side. Don't we all wanna hitch a ride with somebody else if we think it's gonna hike our own status up a notch or two? Who doesn't like standing next to a hero? We all want power. And if we can't get it, then we wanna at least rub shoulders with it once in awhile.

That's why John and I cornered Him alone and told Him—we didn't ask, we told Him flat out—"Listen, we want You to do somethin' for us."

He said, "What's that, boys?"

"We wanna be right next to Ya in all Your glory. One of us on each side."

He didn't get mad. He just got silent. And after a moment, He said, "You don't know what glory is. You think you can do what I'm gonna do for you in Jackson?"

Together we said *(offhandedly)*, "Sure, we can!"

He just locked eyes with us and said, "Then so be it."

(Beat, then) I ain't too sure what it was we actually agreed upon . . . but I know it didn't feel near as glorious as John and I thought it should.

Well, of course, the other fellas got wind of this and they all got their feathers ruffled up about it. Believe it or not, Pete accused us of bein' too big for our britches! Boy, I tell ya, if that wasn't the pot callin' the kettle black! And I told him as much.

Pete says, "Oh, yeah! How'd you and your brother like to be breathin' out your ears!"

"Put up or shut up, Pete! Either way, I'm about to put my fist where your mouth is!"

By now everybody was puttin' in their two cents, "I'm the one He lets keep all the dues!"—"Yeah, but He's been to my house for dinner!"—"But I knew Him first!"—"So? I gave up more than you!"—"Did not!"—"Did too!"—"DID NOT!"—"DID TOO!"

We were all tussling and shoving each other around by now, everything short of fisticuffs. Matt had little Jimmy in a headlock while Tom started scuffling with Bart on the ground. Before we knew it, our little tiff had turned into an all-out brawl.

By the time Jesus got us all separated, we were pretty much all tuckered out, anyway. Only thing really bruised were our egos. I pointed at Pete and yelled, "He started it!" Pete yelled back, "Did not!" (Starting in again) "Did too!" "Did not!" We'd already been down this road, and it hadn't gotten us anywhere. But Jesus just stood there and let us spout off at each other until we finally wound down and shut up.

Jesus sat us all down and said, "You guys are so concerned about power and status. Haven't you heard My words? Don't you know I've come to turn that all upside down? Whichever one of you wants to be the greatest is gonna have to become the least. You want to be raised up, you're gonna have to lie down. You want to receive, you're gonna have to give away. Don't you see? I haven't come to be served but to serve and to pay a debt none of you can afford."

(Sheepishly) Well, we all knew what we had to do. We all kind of brushed each other off and slapped one another on the back and chuckled at our childishness. Although, I do admit Pete and I almost knocked each other back down tryin' to be the first one to help the other one up. Egos are a fragile thing, ain't they?

Anyway, I'm takin' all this food to the boys. Kind of a peace offering, if you will, to the other fellas. Jesus' words are finally sinkin' in a bit. (Gesturing to the food, shrugging good-naturedly) You know, serving others and all.

Although, I ain't too sure I understand about this debt He's gonna pay. But I think that's why we're headin' down to Jackson . . . I think He's gonna show us what He means there.

(Picks up the box of food) In the meantime, this oughta make the boys happy. I ain't too proud to say I'm sorry. (Looking around) The place here seems to be keepin' busy. (Aside to the audience) I guess I better not tell Pa what Jesus can do with a couple filets and hush puppies. It might hurt business. (Smiles and leaves with the order)

23

JOHN

NOTE: Throughout history, John has come to be known as "the disciple whom Jesus loved" or "the beloved." Much of John's character is revealed through his Gospel. In the Book of John there is no mention of the facts of Christ's birth, His baptism, the Temptation, the Transfiguration, or Communion at the disciple's Last Supper, the agony He went through in the garden the night He was arrested, and no mention is made of Christ crying out that God had forsaken Him when He needed Him the most. Jesus does not tell one single parable in the Book of John. What does this say about John?

For John, Jesus is the embodiment of truth. The facts have their place, but they are not as relevant as the truth Jesus demonstrated in His words and actions. Just before He raises Lazarus from the grave, Jesus uses the incident not to declare the fact that He's going to physically raise the dead (an impressive enough feat). But He uses the moment to speak the truth, "I am the resurrection and the life. He who believes in me will live, even though he dies; and whoever lives and believes in me will never die" (11:25-26, NIV).

Christ always drove the truth home with His words. And He backed up His words with His actions. They were one in the same. Truth is like that. John never let the facts stand in the way of the truth. And John loved Jesus not because He healed the ill and fed the hungry but for the eternal truth found within the miracles—that He'd come to save humankind.

(AT RISE: John is dressed casually. He is sitting cross-legged with a legal pad on his lap. He is chewing on a pencil, deep in thought. He is surrounded by crumpled bits of paper. He is an older man, yet full of energy.)

JOHN *(thinks a moment, then as if inspiration has hit, scribbles furiously):* Oh my, better get that gem down before I forget it. That's a beauty! *(Stares at his paper a moment)* All right, let's see what we've got here. *(Reading it back)* "My Memoirs. By John. Chapter One. In the beginning . . ." *(He is obviously stumped, tries it again.)* "In the beginning . . ." *(Trying a more dramatic inflection)* "In the beginning . . ." *(Disheartened, rips page off and tosses it over his shoulder)* Naw, that's no good. It's already been used. *(Paces about)* It's gotta be more of a grabber. Something that'll hit the reader between the eyes! Something that'll reveal who He really was, His true nature! *(Intense)* It's too important not to get it right.

(Speaks directly to the audience) Writer's block, can you believe

it? A title and my name and I'm already stuck. *(Gesturing to his pad)* It's not really my story I'm trying to write, but His *(quick glance upward)*, and how His life changed mine forever. You'd think that wouldn't be so hard. *(Remembering)* Someone who turned my life upside down. Someone I came to love more than life itself.

(Back to audience) But when you're a poet, you weigh every word. You commit Roget's Thesaurus to heart. You try them all until you find just the right one. And, like all good poets, I'm suffering for my art. I've been deported out here to this island because of my beliefs in Him. But, if you gotta pick an island to be banished to, Nantucket's not a bad place. A lot of us poets and writers hang out here, waiting for inspiration to hit. *(Ruefully rubbing his chin)* Some of us die waiting. *(Cheering up)* Oh, and don't forget! Without Nantucket there would be no young girl who got her head stuck in a bucket. *(Chuckles at his wit, abruptly stops)* It's strange how much funnier one is when he's alone.

(Tosses the pad down) Maybe I'm trying too hard. Maybe if I just jump in and tell you some of what happened, inspiration'll come to me. But I don't wanna start at the beginning . . . I'm already stuck for an opener. Let me start with what we all thought was the beginning of the end . . . our last meal together.

When Jesus finished with our feet, and we all settled back for the meal, that's when He dropped the bomb. He was always doing that to us. If we seemed to get a little too comfortable, He'd always say or do something that made us squirm a bit. When He told us that one of us would betray Him, none of us jumped to our feet to contradict Him. Instead we looked around the room at each other, no one really catching anyone else's eye for fear of what they'd see in our own.

Peter whispered to me, "Ask Him who it is."

So I leaned over and asked Him, "Who is it, Lord?"

(Beat, then to audience) Isn't it strange that we all thought it might be us? How else can I explain that even after He'd handed the bread to Judas and told him to do what he had to do, none of us tried to stop him. Maybe that's because none of us could see beyond or own trembling fingers, thankful that the bread wasn't handed to us. Maybe it's because we were all culpable to some degree.

Whatever the reason, Jesus didn't hold it against us. Instead, He comforted us with . . . *(said in wonder)* with words . . . Words that not only soothed our hearts but broke them as well. He spoke of Peter's denial, and in the same breath told us to love each other, as He loved us. *(Finding his way, not fully understanding)* He spoke of truth, and a way, and of life with meaning . . . what all the great poets search for. He made Longfellow and Frost read like nursery rhymes.

He spoke in perfect metaphor about a true vine and a Gardener . . . and about the branches. *(Remembering reverently)* It was pure poetry. And in the same breath that He commanded us to love one another, He called us to lay down our lives for each other. His words were beautiful . . . yet His truths were hard.

He said the world would hate us and that we would grieve and weep and mourn in this life. And in the same breath He said that He would send comfort and that our sorrow would turn to jubilation.

I have known both the anguish and the joy He spoke of . . . the anguish of seeing Him nailed to a tree and the joy of an empty grave.

I've known what it is for my soul to be in torment as He stood before the governor and let himself be sentenced to die. *(Desperately)* You see, I was there! He had the opportunity to save himself. The governor even asked Him if He was a lord over some kingdom.

He answered that His kingdom wasn't of this world. But that He was Lord and it was that truth that He'd come to testify to.

(Pulling the audience in) Now listen closely to what happened next. For it set the world on ear. He asked Jesus, "What is truth?"

(Achingly, drawn out) And Jesus . . . stood . . . silent! . . . And that was His moment! All He had to do was tell him and He could've walked free! Better yet, He could've called on all the armies of heaven to save Him in that moment. But He chose to stand silent.

I did not understand it then, but I do now. For that is the moment we all face, isn't it? Sometime in our lives, we must stare Him in the face and either acknowledge the truth or turn away from it. But either way, it doesn't change. When Pilate stared Truth in the face, it was Pilate's moment to choose . . . not Christ's.

Jesus was more than a great poet. Poets search to find meaning in the chaos of our lives. We search to find a sense of direction or purpose to living. We search for truth. But I have found it. *(With a sense of desperation)* You see, that's what I want to convey to people! The truth of the matter—!

(Stops, stunned at the revelation) Wait a minute! That's it! *(Scrambles to find the last paper he crumpled up, smooths it out and writes frantically)* "In the beginning was the Truth, and the Truth was with God, and the Truth was God . . ."

(Holds it out) That's it! Now I've got something to build on. *(To audience)* And it came to me like a flash, like a . . . a . . . what's the word I'm looking for? . . . *(Snaps his fingers with insight)* A revelation! *(Looking directly at the audience)* Perhaps I'll have more someday . . . *(Smiles in wonder, then begins writing frantically as lights fade quickly)*

PHILIP

NOTE: Although Philip is listed as one of the apostles in all four Gospels, it is only in the Gospel of John that anything is revealed about him. I've chosen to take the incident where Jesus asks Philip how they can feed the 5,000 because Philip's response is a mirror into ourselves. Philip's obvious defeat at the overwhelming task points out so clearly the limitations that we place on Jesus. When circumstances engulf us, our human tendency is to be swept away by the tide. Philip is so busy rolling his eyes at the impossible task that he almost misses the miracle of a little boy in their midst. A lunch. That's all he had to offer, but it was enough. God doesn't want much . . . just everything we've got.

(AT RISE: Philip enters and crosses to center stage. He is wearing a pair of overalls, farmer cap, and workboots. He appears strong, and his face is lined with hard work. He is a farmer. He squats down and lifts up a handful of dirt and examines it.)

PHILIP *(to himself):* He spoke a lot in riddles. A lot of 'em havin' to do with the soil and what type of crops grew best where. *(Letting the dirt fall through his fingers)* I guess that's one o' the reasons I attached myself to Him.

(Rises and brushes his hands off, addresses the audience) The name is Phil. I got 200 acres just north of Logansport. *(Realizing the audience doesn't have a clue where that is)* Which is just west of Boone? . . . *(Rambles the remainder off quickly)* Which is just outside of Ames, which is just outside of Des Moines, Iowa. 28 miles due north of Des Moines, to be exact. Ya'll heard of Des Moines, surely. 'Specially with the flood of '93 and all. Anybody with an idiot box in their livin' room had to have seen that.

The Des Moines River left its banks the first of July, and we packed up and left the farm right on its heels. I'd been through droughts and floods before and, like most farmers, we're a tolerant lot and have learned to wait things out. *(Empty of emotion)* But nothin' compared to the flood of '93. Nate, a friend of mine, took me up in his duster and we did a flyover. Nothin' but the roof of my barn to see and the top of a line of telephone poles. You could just make out where the original banks of the Des Moines had been by the top of the trees cuttin' a scraggly line through the water. At some places, the river was 4 miles wide. I only knew that by countin' the section markers of farmland that were flooded. Down south outside St. Louis, where the Mississippi and the Missouri meet up, it was as much as 17 miles wide.

It seemed that a lot of hope was carried away with those rains. I didn't even see the ground for 2 months. I knew this season was lost, and I'd have to watch the guv'ment hand me checks for not farmin' again. It's a strange country when you can get paid for not doin' what it is your Poppa got paid for doin'.

Now I know God promised Noah that he'd never destroy the world by water again. But then, I guess Noah must not o' been a farmer. My world was purty much washed away, along with all my topsoil and crops. So when the Preacher come through town claimin' to be our salvation, I grabbed Nate and followed Him, lookin' for some answers.

We were all down by the Saylorville Dam throwin' our backs in to sandbaggin' with the rest of the folk. None of us knew whether it was gonna hold or not. But that didn't matter as much as just doin' somethin' to feel useful. Well, there wadn't even enough dry land left for ever'body to stand on so the Preacher paddles out a ways from the bank in a rowboat and starts singin' nursery rhymes to us.

(Singing) "Old MacDonald had a farm. Ei, ei, oh.
And on that farm he sowed some corn. Ei, ei, oh.
With some corn over here, and some corn over there,
On the road, in the rocks, even grew a thorn—corn.
Old Macdonald had a farm. Ei, ei, oh."

That certainly got our attention. Folks stopped long enough to yell at Him, "Why You makin' jokes, Preacher?" "You mockin' our troubles? Is that what You're up to?"

He stood up in the rowboat and said *(with childlike enthusiasm),* "Don't you get it? I'm old MacDonald! And the corn is My message. There some folk among you who hear My message but don't understand it, and they're like the corn growin' along the road. Sooner or later, it gets eaten by crows. In the same way Satan'll snatch it away from you 'cause it don't go deep in your heart.

"Corn growin' among rocks is like some o' you who follow Me 'cause I momentarily take your mind off your troubles. I'm just a distraction from your heartache. But since you got no roots, when the trouble continues, you'll fall away.

"And some o' you are like the corn among the thorns. You let the worries of this life—your house, livestock, possessions, money—choke away those things that are eternal.

"Oh, but some of you here represent good fertile soil. And those of you that hear My words and let it sink into your hearts, why I guarantee you'll produce up to a hundredfold what you sow!

(Compassionately) "I ain't making light of anybody's heartache. That ain't my way. But those of you who got ears—and I ain't talkin' corn now, I hope you're listenin'. 'Cause I'm askin' you, which kinda soil are ya gonna be?"

(Beat, then) Maybe it was the rain runnin' off the end of our noses, maybe it was the way our clothes kept stickin' to our skin. But we'd had enough. *(Angry)* "Don't talk to us about soil! I'd like to be able to see dry ground again!" *(Incredulously)* "We been muckin' about in this mud fightin' to hold on to our very lives while You sing songs at us!"

(Talking to audience) We got strong backs, but they'd been broken by all this rain, and He'd pushed us too far. *(Shaking his head sadly)* I guess we just didn't get it. We couldn't see who He was for all the sweat runnin' in our eyes. Couple days later, we we're all still at it . . . fillin' bags, sandbaggin' walls. Tryin' to beat the inevitable. We'd been workin' all day, and it was comin' on toward suppertime. And the Preacher comes over to me and says, "Phil, look at all these hungry folk. How in the world are we gonna get enough bread to feed 'em all?"

(Put out) Now, why He chose to ask me such a stupid question, I'll never know. Surely, He must've known how I'd answer. *(Sparing nothing)* "What kind of a dumb, dopey, brainless, ignorant, thick-headed question is that, Preacher? I got 200 acres of cream of wheat! I got a year's wages under water! We'll be doin' good to see pocket change around here!"

'Bout then Charlie Barne's little boy, Elroy, pushes my leg aside and steps forward holdin' out his sack lunch; a bologna sandwich and a can of sardines. It wasn't much. *(Beat)* But it turned out to be enough. The Preacher sets us all down and blesses the lunch and starts passin' it around. *(Still not believing it, stumped)* Well, somehow it just kept gettin' passed around 'til ever'body was full up! We even had leftovers for a snack later on.

The Preacher just looks at us all sittin' around pickin' our teeth and says, "You gettin' it now, folks? You just gotta bring Me what you got. I'll always make it enough. I know a kind of bread that, come what may, will always fill you up."

We all clamored to be heard at once. "Give us that grain, Preacher!" "I'll plant my whole farm with it!"

He looks us over and says, "I'm it. I'm the *real* wonder bread. Don't just sweat and toil your whole life for an acre of food that the sun can beat down and wither in a day, or that the rains can wash away in one night. But remember there's food that's eternal, which I've come to give you. If you come to Me, you'll never go hungry. If you believe in Me, you'll never be thirsty. *I* am the bread of life. You gettin' it now, folks?"

And I did. It finally sunk in. *(With a sense of awe)* The Son of God was in our midst. And He'd come to do more than just help us keep our heads above water . . . He'd come to help us walk on it. He'd come to do more than help us drudge through the muck of our circumstances . . . He'd come to lift us out of it.

(To audience) What about you, folks? Got any rivers you can't cross? You 'bout to go under? Your levee 'bout to break? 'Cause I can guarantee ya, it will.

(Squats down and picks up a handful of dirt again) So, I guess the question is—What kinda dirt are ya? Does your faith in Him go deep? Will your roots hold, no matter the situation? 'Cause there's no tellin' what can grow in fertile soil. *(Locks eyes with audience)* You gettin' it now, folks? *(Blackout)*

NATHANAEL

NOTE: Tradition has it that Nathanael was a scribe of the Jewish law. According to the Gospel of John, Nathanael was the first to recognize Jesus as the Son of God, not just as the Messiah they had so long awaited but as the embodiment of their Lord. It is somewhat ironic that just three verses prior to Nathanael's insight he almost casually dismisses Jesus in an offhanded way simply because of where Philip says Jesus comes from. "Nazareth! Can anything good come from there?" Even Nathanael had the all-too-human tendency to dismiss others before even meeting them, based solely on prejudice or personal inclination. Oh, but what great miracles and wonders did Nathanael almost miss because of it! What miracles and workings of Jesus might we miss given our predisposition toward those around us?

(AT RISE: Nathanael is seated behind a desk that is piled high with textbooks. We cannot see him, but if we could we would see that he is wearing a very preppy suit and tie. He has glasses on his nose and has that scholarly air of academia about him. He is a bookish student in his 20s and speaks with an English accent.)

NATHANAEL *(seated behind a huge stack of textbooks on a desk; we cannot see him but we hear his voice; as each title is read, he sets that textbook to the side, slowly revealing himself buried behind the books):* "Biblical Hermeneutics: A Concise Guide to the Method and Principles of Scriptural Interpretation." *(Sets book aside, picks up another)* "Old Testament Eschatology." *(Does the same again)* "The Philosophies of Religion." *(And again)* "The Dead Sea Scrolls and Its Theology." *(Begins picking up his pace)* "Theological Anthropology," "Process Philosophy and Theology." *(Rattling them off quickly now)* "The Philosophy of Theology," "The Theology of Philosophy," and "The Philosophical Theology Found in Philosophy."

    (Stacks the last book, revealing himself, smiles broadly, takes a deep breath and says) Hello, there. I'm a religion major. Actually, I've been working toward my doctorate in religious education. I'm on a fellowship here at Cambridge. I'm also one of the youngest TAs *(clarifying for those that might not know)*, teaching assistants, Cambridge University has ever had.

    (Rises, and crosses downstage with an air of condescension) Let me explain. You see, Cambridge University consists of over 20 semiautonomous colleges. Each student is assigned a tutor, who becomes the keystone of the college system here at Cambridge. This tutor is

both the student's mentor and the chief link between the student and the college. My current mentor has me transcribing various passages of text for him from the original Greek.

Cambridge University is one of the oldest institutions of higher education in England. It was founded in the early years of the 13th century. And to my way of thinking, that was the last time a new thought had entered its courtyards. There are times when I believe the only thing more stuffy than its hallowed halls would be King Tut's tomb. And even that's had an airing out.

Perhaps that is why I did much of my studying outside, sitting beneath a tree found just outside the courtyard of Trinity College. *(With conviction)* I kept looking for a new insight, a new way of conveying the old truths found in Scripture. Many of us here were looking for a new hope. But if all else failed, I could do as many before me had done—spend my days holed up in some institution of higher learning, or perhaps even a monastery, meditating on the religions of the world, reading philosophy, and studying the great minds of religious thought. But, thank God, I got up from underneath my tree! But I almost didn't.

When Philip came running toward me and said, "He's here, old boy! There's a new religion professor on campus. And He's the one we've been waiting for ever since Moses!" It was with a healthy degree of skepticism I listened. You see, we students have a tendency to indulge ourselves in anything new. Part of the college experience, I imagine. But I thought to myself, "Could this actually be the One I've waited for?" But Philip's next words made my heart sink. "He's a guest lecturer. *(Excited with the novelty of it)* And He's from America!"

(With great disdain) "America! Can anything good come from America?" I said. A country who's great intellect has given us the cheeseburger and professional wrestling didn't exactly cause my spirits to soar.

Philip just ran off yelling, "Come and see for yourself!" Which I did.

(He tucks a book under his arm, and crosses the stage.) I left the shade of my tree, with my books tucked under my arm *(cynical)* and went in search of this great teacher from America. While I was still a ways off, He spotted me across the green and said, "Here comes a true believer, a man whose soul intent is to discover truth."

I slowed my steps as I approached Him. "How do You know what my soul intent is?"

He answered, "Because I saw you underneath your tree with your nose in your books before Philip even called to you."

(Taken aback, to audience) But how did He know what I was reading? How did He know that I had spent the last six years of

academia poring over the ancient tomes of the history of man, studying what the great minds of the world had to say about life, searching and praying for the ultimate truth to be revealed to me! *(Said with disgust)* How did this American, this person of questionable origin from some podunk place across the water come to know my mind? *(With a sense of mystery)* His knowledge couldn't have come from a book.

(With a newfound sense of respect) "Professor!" I said. "Surely You're more than just a guest orator on philosophy? You're more than a master or fellow of religion, aren't You? You're the Son of God; the embodiment of truth."

He said to me, "You believe that because I saw you under a tree? There's more to it than Me simply reading your mind. You'll see greater wonders than that!"

I attached myself to Him for the next few days. He even went with me over to my hometown in the borough of Leeds one weekend. Several of us were there to see a friend married off. Little did I realize it would be the first of many wonders I would see at the hands of the Professor. The wedding went off without a hitch. It was at the reception where the social obligations of the family began to run dry, if you get my drift. It seems they ran out of Rosy Glow punch.

Before a serious faux pas could occur, the Professor said to go ahead and just fill the punchbowl from the tap in the kitchen. The servants did as He suggested, and I'll be confounded if the water didn't taste like Rosy Glow punch! Everyone was busy pulling the groom aside and congratulating him not on his choice of bride but on his witty stratagem of saving the best punch till now!

But I knew there was more than turning water into wine going on here. I searched out the Professor and He looked at me with a gleam in His eye. *(Smiling)* And this time I read *His* mind. I knew the Professor was suggesting that the best was now standing before me, that He had come to introduce a new way of learning. Not to replace the old truths but to fulfill them. *(With a sense of awe and wonder)* And that the angels of God had sent down truth to us in this man.

And from that moment on, I have put my books down and put my faith in Him. I don't know what is to come. I don't imagine He'll last too long around here. His words are much too radical for this place. I know He has come to the attention of the chancellor. And that's never a good sign. He doesn't seem to fit in too well with the faculty. I don't think He'll ever get tenure.

But what does it matter? I shall follow Him wherever it leads. For I have a new tutor and mentor now. And to think I almost stayed underneath my tree . . . *(Tosses the book in his hand to the floor)* Who knows? Perhaps there are greater wonders yet to see. *(Exits)*

MATTHEW

NOTE: The Book of Matthew is the only Gospel that gives us what has come to be known as the Sermon on the Mount. Although portions of the Beatitudes are found in Luke as well, it is only Matthew that records the sermon as if it all happened on one occasion. Opinions differ as to whether the sermon is a compilation of the teachings of Jesus on numerous occasions or if Jesus in fact said it all on one occurrence. I have chosen to use the latter in this monologue.

I have also chosen to use the parable of the Pharisee and the publican found in Luke 18:10-14 as the basis for the story Jesus tells Matthew regarding the Rabbi and the tax collector. Interestingly enough, Matthew does not record this parable.

(AT RISE: Matthew is seated at a table busily typing on a notebook computer. He is wearing a suitcoat and tie. He is also wearing a pair of Levi's jeans and tennis shoes, but they aren't visible to the audience until he stands up. From behind the table or desk he appears to be dressed conservatively. He glances up and addresses the audience.)

MATTHEW: Be right with you, just want to get this down before I forget it. *(Types rapidly and then leans back, content)* There . . . perfect. *(Smiles at audience)* That's always been one of my problems. You see, I like to get everything exactly right. I'm a perfectionist. You might find that ironic seeing as how I also work for the government. It's like the old joke, "You work for the government? How many people work in your department?" "Oh, about half of them." Or the one, "I've been employed by the government for 25 years . . . and I've actually worked 10 of 'em."

But not too many jokes like that surface in my department. There's not a lot of laughing in my division, but it's not unusual to see tears. You see, I work for the Internal Revenue Service here in New York. And we take our job very seriously. I'm known for holding to the letter of the law. I've gained quite a reputation, in fact, for my ability to take those loopholes and turn them into nooses. Around the office they called me "the hanging auditor." That's how I managed to become director of my division so quickly. That's why I have an office on the fifth floor with a view of the fountain by the parking lot. But that's not what I want to talk about. I want to tell you how I lost all that. *(Crosses to corner of desk and sits on it)*

One day last summer the A.C. went on the blink in our entire building. By noon I was still sitting in my office listening to some guy drone on trying to justify his Winnebago as a business expense when I happened to glance out my window and see this man sitting by the fountain, just dangling His toes in the water. That's not so unusual here in New York on a hot day, but of all the windows in this building, this guy was looking right up at mine. He was just sitting there, kicking His feet and grinning up at me! Just smiling away and motioning for me to come on down and join Him.

Maybe it was the heat, maybe it was the wimpering excuses of the man on the other side of my desk. Whatever it was, I leaned out my window and yelled, "Be right there!" You see, if I'm honest with you . . . working for the IRS kinda limits your friends. Nobody wants to get to know you too well. But I figured this guy must not know me from Adam.

By the time I got out the revolving door, He's standing there with these sandals slung over His shoulder saying, "Come on. Follow Me." *(Stands and crosses downstage)*

Well, we struck up a conversation, and I asked Him where He was from, where He lived, what He did for a living. And I noticed His answers were real evasive. He said He wasn't from around here, that He lived wherever men let Him, and that He didn't make much money in His line of work. Maybe it was my nature, but I figured this guy was a prime target for an audit. So I asked Him if He'd ever filed a tax return. I told Him, "It's the law, you know." And He told me He was more interested in the heart of man than in the letter of the law. So by now I figured I had this guy nailed. So I asked Him what tax bracket He was in. He said He really didn't know, that we're all kinda in the same bracket as far as He saw it. Then He went on to tell me about some plan His dad implemented where everybody was supposed to give a flat 10 percent right across the board. *(Smiling and shaking his head condescendingly)* But government being government, I told Him that was much too simple. He laughed and told me I took my job much too seriously, that I should learn to loosen my Windsor knot, maybe trade in my power suit for a pair of 501s. I looked at this ragtag guy and said, "We can't all be indigents, just living from hand to mouth, always expecting a handout. Some of us have to take our jobs seriously. What kind of world would this be if we all just dangled our toes in fountains?"

He just smiled at me and said, "You know what a tax collector with a sense of humor is?" I said no. He said, "Unemployed." I wasn't amused. He sighed and said, "Look, Matt, the bottom line isn't line 64 on a 1040. You see, I'm here to cancel all debts. I want you to realize that in My Father's eyes you're worth far more than just your net assets."

I said, "Could you stop with all the riddles, Jesus. That's the beauty in a column of numbers. There's no morality involved; they either add up or they don't." *(To the audience)* That was the thing with this man, He never shot straight from the hip. He always spoke in riddles. I asked Him why He couldn't just say what was on His mind instead of making jokes and telling stories. He said, "Anybody can preach; you've got thousands of preachers around you. Has it made any difference? Ah, but a good story . . . that stays with you. How many sermons can you remember?"

He had a point there. And to prove it He told me another joke. *(Warming to his story)* "It seems there were these two Jews—a rabbi and a tax collector, and they both headed over to the synagogue to pray one day. Well, the rabbi goes right up to the front of the synagogue where everyone can see him and he begins exhorting *(paces and rants)*, 'Thank God I'm not like everybody else—the murderers in Harlem, adulterers in Brooklyn and Queens, the thieves on Wall Street,' and here the rabbi looks right at the tax collector in the back of the hall and points a righteous finger and growls, 'or the worst of the lot, revenuers! Look at all I do for You, God; I hold to the letter of the law, I skip meals for You, I give You 10% of all that comes in the plate, I don't smoke, I don't chew, and I don't go with women who do!'" *(Ends with a flourish)*

I said, "So what's the punch line, Jesus?" and He said, "I'm not there yet. Hang on, Matt."

Then He goes on to say, "Well, by now the IRS man feels pretty low. He doesn't even darken the door of the place. He just slumps down on the steps outside and lets his chin fall on his chest, and mutters an apology to God, 'I'm worse than lawyers, Lord. Please have mercy on me.'"

Then Jesus just stared at me and shot straight from the hip. *(Gently)* "Here's the punch line, Matt. I want you to know that the tax collector went home forgiven while the rabbi just went home."

(Beat, then smiling) And that was it . . . that's when I began to see what was really important. Several of us have been tagging along with this guy ever since. As you can see, I haven't lost the entire suit yet, but I have traded in the slacks for a pair of jeans. *(Chuckles)* Some of the guys have even started calling me Levi for short. And I've traded in my Florsheims for a pair of Keds. Sandals would be even better—easier getting them on and off whenever we stop to dangle our toes in a fountain. *(Crosses back to corner of desk)*

I've seen some incredible things: miracles, marvels, and wonders. *(Stops and turns to audience)* But the most amazing wonder has happened in here *(tapping his chest)*. But the thing that's really stayed with me isn't the healings, or the feeding of thousands, or even the dead coming to life again. After all, that's just a metaphor for me. *(With passion and intensity)* But it's His *words.* They are so life-changing!

(Turns back to his desk) As you can see, I've still got my notebook computer. But I have traded in my Lotus spreadsheet for WordPerfect. You see, Jesus says some real gems *(gets excited),* like this sermon He gave in Central Park the other day. Somebody's gotta get that all down just exactly right. It's really worth saving. *(Goes back to his computer)*

Now, where was I? Oh, yeah . . . *(begins typing)* "Blessed are the poor in spirit, for they shall be rich in heaven. Blessed are those that grieve, for they will be comforted. Blessed are the gentle, for they will inherit the earth . . ." *(Looks up and smiles at audience)* This is really good, isn't it? I think people will want to remember it someday. *(Continues typing as lights fade)*

THOMAS

NOTE: Thomas, throughout the years, has come to represent the skeptical aspect of man. He has come to be viewed as a man with limited imagination: a realist who accepted only the facts, not hearsay or rumors. In looking for a contemporary profession that would breed such skepticism, what better occupation for Thomas than that of a cynical, seasoned, liberal journalist covering politics on Capitol Hill?

Thomas seemed unable to grasp the divine nature of Jesus. He understood His death clearly enough. After all, he saw that—the facts were indisputable. But when it came time to grasp the miracle of the Resurrection, Thomas wasn't even with the other disciples when Jesus first appeared to them. But Jesus, ever patient and loving, appeared again for Thomas's behalf. And only after Thomas not only saw but grasped the ruined hands of Jesus did he also grasp the reality of God incarnate in Him.

How many miracles happen around us today that we do no grasp because we, too, are like Thomas, refusing to believe anything other than what we see or touch for ourselves?

PRODUCTION NOTE: Update the names of the news media and the political figures, as is needed, to keep them relevant.

(AT RISE: Thomas is standing center stage. He is slightly disheveled looking. He is dressed in a rather crumpled suit. His tie is loose around his neck and his suitcoat is thrown casually over his shoulder. His shirt is wrinkled and his sleeves are rolled up to his forearms. He is a seasoned journalist who has covered politics on Capitol Hill for over a decade. He has an ironic smile and a rather bemused expression on his face.)

THOMAS *(to the audience):* Isn't it ironic? After having seen and reported on all the miracles He did, I still chose not to believe in the greatest one. I guess it's just my nature. Pretty much comes with the job, I suppose. I'm a news correspondent for one of the wire services. I've covered the Hill for over a decade now, so I guess it's no surprise I don't believe everything I hear. Up here rhetoric is everybody's stock in trade. The only things more plentiful than words up here are lawyers. People banter them around kinda like flies at a picnic . . . you keep swatting at them but there's still plenty for everybody.

I mean, look at Reagan. Eight years of words and press conferences and if you ask me today what's one important thing he said . . .

I draw a blank. Kinda like he did at the Iran-Contra hearings. I guess I've pretty much seen and heard it all.

So I wasn't surprised when I heard about the poor boy from Bethlehem, Pa., making His way around the beltway wanting to take His shot at being the next president. I thought *(snickering),* Sure, why not? We look for a new messiah every four years in this country. He can't be any worse than what we've had. *(Caustic)* Hey, if a movie star is qualified to run this country, then why not a steelworker?

And, of course, with any new face on the Hill who might actually have a chance at the White House there was an initial buzz surrounding the Man. People came out of the woodwork to align themselves with Him, just in case His star might rise.

Well, we of the news media had seen all this before. So we just bided our time and waited for Him to trip over His own tongue. Given enough time, all politicians eventually do that. In fact, that's my job—to be there when it happens. You see, Capitol Hill is kinda like a pool full of goldfish. And us—well, we're like the only piranha in the pool. Sooner or later, we're gonna feed on somebody. It didn't take long for us to start nibbling around.

(As if at a press conference, facing stage left) "Mr. Christopher, UPI. What do you plan to do about the homeless and the poor?"

(Facing stage right) "I say we feed them."

(Turning back to stage left) "That seems a little naive, Mr. Christopher. How will that solve the problem?"

(Stage right) "It won't. You'll always have the hungry. But that's no argument to neglect them. I say feed the ones in front of you. *(Gestures to someone else)* Yes, over there."

(À la Sam Donaldson) "Yes, ABC here. Mr. Christopher, how do you stand on taxes?"

(Smiling good-naturedly) "Now, Mr. Donaldson, you're not gonna trap me with that one. Who's on a quarter, Sam?"

(À la Sam Donaldson) "Aren't You avoiding the issue, Sir—!"

(Gently interrupting him) "Who's on a quarter, Sam?"

"Why, Mr. George Washington, of course!"

"Then why don't you take that quarter and go give him a call and give him what you owe him. Next question . . ."

(Back to the audience) Well, Sam's eyeballs got as big as his ego and for the first time we watched that vulcan eyebrow of his shoot *up!* Needless to say, we were impressed. Anybody who could make Sam shut up was worth paying attention to.

So, I got myself permanently assigned to Him. *(With an air of condescension)* I kept waiting to see through His smokescreen. But He seemed to actually want to make a difference in people's lives. I think that's why He seemed so popular at first with the working man. He certainly didn't speak like a politician. None of the lobbyists seemed to know how to approach Him. One guy from GM asked Him point blank, "Look, what've I gotta do to get You in our pocket?"

He said, "Start by selling off your profits and giving them away. You do that, then we can talk. You see, you got about as much chance of getting Me in your pocket, as you do of entering the kingdom of God." *(Admiringly)* This guy made Ross Perot look like a pussycat!

I kept close to Mr. Christopher, waiting to see His real intentions. You see, He never really declared a party line. Just talked about a plan of reform for everybody: Republican and Democrat, Black and White, rich and poor. Then He started showing His true colors and demonstrating His aid package. You see, He began solving the health-care problem on His own by giving sight to the blind, healing the crippled, and curing the incurable. He never billed anybody for His services. This didn't sit too well with the AMA. People started canceling their insurance policies. They didn't seem to need them anymore, as long as He was around.

He talked about solving the national debt by simply canceling it. "Forgive your debtors, as I've forgiven you." He talked about a flat tax rate of 10 percent for everybody, although He didn't call it tax. He called it tithing, said it'd been around since the beginning of time.

These kinds of statements made headlines, of course! And enemies. Banks, savings and loans, and every financial institution in America started pounding on the doors of Congress. "Shut Him up! Our economy will collapse! We've got to impeach Him!"

But how are you gonna impeach someone who's not even been elected? I knew His aid package was just pie in the sky. In practicality, it would never work. But so what? That's how you get elected in this country! You say whatever you need to . . . you just don't say "Read my lips."

(Slightly incredulous) But He seemed intent on presenting this scheme of His to Congress. I told Him, "You carry this plan of Yours up the hill and Congress'll crucify it!"

But that didn't seem to bother Him. "Don't let that trouble you. I'll take care of everything. *(Smiling like a politician)* Trust Me."

(Full of cynicism and doubt, addressing imaginary Mr. Christopher) "Trust You! Oh, that's a good one! That's the oldest joke up here, next to Jesse Helms. How can I trust You? I've been covering the Hill too long to trust anybody! That's the first thing that goes up here. You can't believe anything you hear and only half of what you see!"

"Believe this, Thomas. I am the way, the truth, and the life. If you can believe that, then follow Me."

(Speaking to the audience again) Well, I knew it was a story, so I

strung along. But I knew where the lead would end. I'd seen it a hundred times before. And believe it or not, the whole town was glued to C-Span while Congress shot Him and His aid package full of holes. Some old soldier offered to bury Him in a tomb in Arlington.

And that was pretty much it. Like all our hope, He was put down by the greedy and the powerful. Nothing left to write but the byline. I guess some of the boys headed for the local watering hole to relive it. But not me. I had a story to file.

A few days later I was sitting over by the Lincoln Memorial, feeling low and chastising myself for buying into Mr. Christopher's Camelot in the first place when Sam comes running alongside the reflecting pool yelling (*à la Sam Donaldson again*), "He's alive, Tom! We've seen Him! He's got Dan and Peter dancing on the tables for joy! Even Koppel's smiling. Come on!"

(*Shaking his head sadly at such naïveté*) I couldn't believe it. "Sam, what has happened to you? Where's your objectivity? Have you lost sight of the facts? What you're saying is impossible!"

"I know that, Tom. But I'll eat my toupee if it isn't true!"

Well, that was worth seeing and I told him as much.

"Unless I see the holes they blasted in Him with my own eyes . . . no, better yet, unless I put my finger in those holes I won't believe it!"

A week later, Sam was still wearing his toupee and I ate humble pie in front of the boys. When He walked into the room and turned to face me, Mr. Christopher said, "Go ahead, Tom. Don't believe your eyes. Put your finger here." And I'm sad to say I did. And only then did I really believe and fall on my face before God.

(*Not quite so glib*) Now, don't you find that ironic? I know *He* did, and He said as much. "Tom, how many times did you watch Me give sight to the blind. Yet you, who've seen these miracles with your own eyes, still stumble around in the dark. Blessed are those who believe in Me without seeing."

(*Takes a beat, then looks at audience*) Those were the last words He said to me . . . but they were meant for you. And I wonder how many miracles we miss because we don't see them? Or how many of our prayers He answers that we don't acknowledge? Or how many angels protect us that go unnoticed? Or how many blessings surround us that we never recognize? (*Urgently and sincerely*) Don't miss the miracles!

How many times did my "cynical" nature blind me from seeing the miraculous? I don't know . . . Maybe there's a little bit of me in all of us. You may only see me as the skeptic, the one who always demanded proof. And you may say, "I will never be like that." I hope so and pray you are right. Maybe it *was* just me . . . (*looks directly at the audience and smiles*) but I doubt it. (*Blackout*)

THE OTHER JAMES

NOTE: Scripture does little more than give us the name of the other James. In Mark, he is referred to as "James the less." Whether this is in regard to physical stature or age, we can only theorize. The Greek word means "little" or "short," so I've chosen to interpret it as a physical trait. Some believe that James' father, Alphaeus, was Joseph of Nazareth's brother. If that is so, then there is some basis to believe that James and Jesus were cousins. I've chosen to use this theory for the basis of the following monologue. James may have been viewed as "little" by those around him, but Jesus saw that his heart was big enough. And little becomes much in the hands of Jesus.

(AT RISE: James is short, 5'5" to be exact. He makes up for what he lacks in height by his agility and enthusiasm for the game. He is very quick and athletic; he's just short. He is wearing casual workout clothes, sweats and tennis shoes. He also carries a well-worn football. He is anywhere from 20 to 35 years old. Age doesn't matter as much as exuberance.)

JAMES *(he is center stage facing the audience in a quarterback stance holding a football awaiting the hike from the imaginary center, looks right and left, calling out the snap-count):* "28-39-16-7-7-hut! hut! hut!" *(Falls a step or two back as if to pass the ball, surveys the field, à la announcer voice)* There's the snap! He fades back into the pocket! He's pressured from every side! He's looking for a receiver! Time is running down! 5-4-3 . . . ! *(Cocks the ball behind his head and lets an imaginary pass fly)* He's thrown a Hail Mary, folks! This is for the game! It's . . . ! It's . . . ! CAUGHT! 20-15-10-5-TOUCHDOWN! It's all over! A 75-yard touchdown pass! Little Jimmy does it again! *(He is jumping all over in delirium.)* How did he do it, people! Jimmy has just led his team to another super bowl victory! This will undoubtably go down in history as one of the greatest comebacks ever! I tell you, Jimmy may be the smallest man to ever play the game, but right now he's gotta be the biggest man out there. For my money, he's one of the greatest quarterbacks to ever play the game!

   (Makes crowd noises and then fades them out, smiles and addresses audience casually, tossing the football) Well, we can all dream, can't we? At 5'5", 155 pounds dripping wet, I know I'm no Joe Montana. And I know I'll never be the greatest to ever play the game. That would have to be my cousin, Jess.

   You see, I grew up with my dad constantly putting me in a

headlock and giving me a noogie while shouting *(boisterously)*, "Jimmy, my boy! Go out for a pass!" I always had good hands, but I was always short too. And inevitably the ball would sail a couple feet over my head. Dad would hang his head in disgust and snort, "Why can't you be more like Joe's boy? He's got a scholarship to play ball at Michigan State, you know." *(Tired of hearing about it)* Believe me, I knew.

(Explaining) Joe was my uncle, my dad's brother. And his son, Jess, was the bane of my existence growing up. It wasn't that I didn't like my cousin. *(Disgusted)* It was just that anything I could do . . . He could do better.

The year we were in wood shop together, I carved this really nifty salad spoon and he made this 10-foot-high cross. When I asked Him what He was doing, He just said, "My father's business." He was always saying weird things like that and stumping everybody at school, even His teachers.

(Full of admiration) But, boy! Could He throw the pigskin. All through high school, while I sat on the bench and listened to my dad chanting from the stands, "Gimme Jimmy! Gimme Jimmy! Gimme Jimmy!" Jess would be throwing touchdown passes and setting records. He had the golden arm. Anything Jess threw up for grabs was always caught. The only thing I ever threw up was my lunch in fear of actually being called on to play.

Even in college I would've needed a stepladder to get underneath the center. I'd reached my whole height of 65 inches. And it was still less than the circumference of some of those guys' necks. And while they grew up watching Chuck Connors of "The Rifleman," I was always rooting for Little Joe on "Bonanza." I loved the game, but I obviously drew the short straw. I never thought I'd ever get the chance to play. So, as the years went by, I grew pretty comfortable watching Jess play pro ball on Sunday afternoons. It was enough to say He was my cousin. I thought it was, anyway. But He had other plans for me.

When He called me from training camp in mid-July I thought it was a joke. *(Holds imaginary phone to his ear)* "Little Jimmy, I need you. Get on down here as fast you can."

"You need me? You're joking, right? I'm still 5'5", you know . . ."

"I'm not interested in your height. I'm interested in your heart."

(Chuckling) "My heart? There's plenty of guys with heart who're sitting on the sidelines."

"Cousin, you wanna get in the game or not?"

(To audience) I knew it took more than heart to play the game. But I thought, Why not? Maybe this was my shot at something bigger.

I got to know the boys pretty well by midseason. We seemed to be a pretty good team. Oh sure, there were the usual problems as far as egos go. Any time you get that much talent together, you're gonna have some problems. Our star backs were the Zebedee brothers, Jim and John. They seemed to always be bickering among themselves and vying for starting running back. They were always squabbling over who got more yards per carry, who got more carries per game, who got the higher salary. Sibling rivalry, I guess. Anyway, these guys had thighs bigger than my waist. They were known throughout the league as "Thunder Thighs."

We also had a star wide receiver, Pete Barjona. We just called him "Bargin' Pete." Sometimes, he talked a better game than he played. He had a tendency to fumble now and then. And he was always having run-ins with the press. But everybody knew that Jess would go to Pete for the long one. And Jess expected Pete to carry the ball on in.

Where did I fit in on this team? (Holds up his hands and smiles) I had steady hands, remember? So I handled the snap on extra points. I held the ball while somebody else got the glory for kicking it through the uprights. Not near as glamorous, but that was OK. I was finally in the game.

That final season we were looking pretty good. We were finally coming together as a team, and we'd reached the playoffs. Jess had His own style and some of us never got real comfortable with it. He always called His own plays. And He never hesitated to call an audible at the line of scrimmage. We wondered how this all sat with the offensive coach up in the booth. And several of the boys wanted to see the head coach. Jess just told us, "When you see Me, you've seen the coach."

Well, come playoff time we even had the home-field advantage. We were all feeling pretty good about that. But in the locker room before the game Jess said (pacing about, this is His Knute Rockne speech), "Men, I want you all to know something. And it's the God's honest truth. Every one of you can do what I've been doing. In fact, you'll do greater things than what I've done! And I don't care what your size is, or what your abilities are . . . if you'll only believe in Me. For you see, things are gonna change now. Sure, they love us now as long as we're winning. But the minute I get sacked—and it's gonna happen—they won't know My name. So I expect you to pick up the ball now."

We all told Him to a man that that would never happen! We'd all protect Him. And then to a man, we all failed.

I'll never forget that game. Nothing seemed to be working. Somehow the opposition knew our every move. Jess'd call an audible at the line, and still they'd know to blitz. It looked pretty bad.

The Sons of Thunder both left the game, one with a twisted ankle and the other with a pulled tendon. Even Pete pulled himself outta the game after his third fumble.

We all stood on the sidelines and watched 'em sack Jess for the umpteenth time. We knew He wouldn't get up from that last one. We watched them carry Him off on a stretcher, and we knew Jess had played His last game. And us . . . ? Well, we knew without Jess we were out for the season. Most of us were placed on injury reserve.

We found out later that the opposition had offered one of our own players some extra incentives—cash, Ferrari, a Nike endorsement—if he'd sell us out before the game. Seems he gave all our plays to the other team. Last I heard, he never got that Nike endorsement. Seems he hung up his cleats for good.

But the rest of us recovered from that season. They couldn't even keep Jess down. He came back to coach each one of us on to greater things, just like He said. We never all played ball together again like that season. And even though we all went different ways, with Jess's help we pretty much changed the game forever.

You see, we've all continued to carry the ball for Him, just like He asked us to. And I've come to see what He meant by heart and not height. He never measured me by what I could or couldn't do. He only measured me by how much I wanted to get in the game.

(Casually starts tossing the ball again, looking at the audience) How 'bout you? You carrying the ball? Or are you still sitting and just watching on Sundays? *(He assumes the quarterback stance again, takes the imaginary snap and falls a step or two back as if to pass the ball, surveys the audience, à la announcer voice again.)* There's the snap! He fades back into the pocket! He's pressured from every side! He's looking for a receiver! Time is running down! 5-4-3 . . . ! *(Cocks the ball behind his head as if to pass to the audience, quick blackout)*

THADDEUS

> NOTE: Very little is known of Thaddeus. In fact, he only appears in the listing of the 12 apostles in the Gospels of Matthew and Mark. He is not referred to in the Scriptures again. Hence, there is little scriptural evidence on which to base him. However, there is a legend that Thaddeus healed the king of Edessa of a disease that medical science had been unable to cure. Hence, there is the slightest of possibilities that Thaddeus might've been a doctor. Given that tenuous premise, I have based Thaddeus's occupation, a medical student, on that sole legend. It is intriguing to imagine how a young doctor might've reacted to Jesus—this Man who healed and cured, not with a license, but with the name of God.

(AT RISE: Thaddeus is wearing a doctor's lab coat. A stethoscope is in one pocket. He carries a clipboard with someone's health chart attached. He is pleasant-looking, any age after 30.)

THADDEUS *(looking at the clipboard):* Everything seems to be fine . . . blood pressure normal, no weight gain, blood count is good . . . *(Looks up at audience)* Pardon me? *(Listens)* To be perfectly frank, I'm not really sure how I ended up being a doctor. Even as a kid, I hated the sight of blood. Especially my own. *(Closing the health chart)* A broken toenail would make me queasy. I was the only kid in elementary school who carried Band-Aids in case he had an accident. I remember when my best friend, Alan Codneys, got hit on the head with a rock. I was the one who fainted. He covered it up with a washcloth and ran five blocks to my house just to watch me pass out.

When my mom told me she was pregnant with my little sister, I immediately threw up. I kept doing it every morning for the next two months. Mom felt fine. I was the one with morning sickness. Maybe that's why I always wanted to be a doctor. I've always hated pain. It never mattered whether it was mine or not. And if I'm honest, perhaps I wanted to be a doctor to get over my fear of that.

Believe me, there are worse reasons to become a doctor. *(Confidingly)* One of my classmates in medical school wanted to be a doctor just for the sense of power it gave him. Not over life and death, but the power of just being able to keep people waiting for hours in a small room. So, of course, he chose pediatrics. Last I heard, he was doing very well for himself. Painted his whole house in primary colors, though.

Most of my skills I learned after med school. For three years I did my residency at Bethany General under a Dr. Christopher. He was incredible. He handled everything: skin disorders, blindness, spinal injuries, paralysis, the hearing impaired, paraplegics. *(Smiling)* "Physically challenged" is the politically correct term, I believe. He even handled three code blues. They were as good as dead until Dr. Christopher stepped in. *(Remembering)* Let's see, there was that widow lady's boy, there was that church deacon's little girl, and who could forget Mr. Lazarus. They'd already taken him down to the morgue.

Actually, there were four code blues if I count Dr. Christopher himself. Nobody seemed to know what He was lecturing about when He said, "Physician, heal yourself." But I guess He pretty much showed everybody what He meant by that.

How He did all this is beyond me. And that's OK. I've seen too many things happen that can't be explained by medical science. He would take all these suffering people who were broken and dying and somehow He would make them whole again. I'm not talking just about the miraculous physical healings. I'm talking about the spirit, the soul inside each of us. You see, His bedside manner healed as many people as did His skills.

He never hesitated to make house calls. I know many physicians have forsaken that just as soon as they realized it wasn't part of the Hippocratic Oath. But He said it was what He was here to do. A lot of people were put off by it. He'd just show up, knock on the door, and wait to be asked in. Some folks didn't care for a checkup and would bolt the door instead. I think they did it mainly out of fear.

In spite of all His abilites, He considered himself a heart specialist. He said there was nothing He liked more than doing open-heart surgery on folks. Too many people walking around with a weak pulse, shallow breathing, and heart murmurs.

One such man was a Mr. Nick DeMuss. He'd been in and out of the hospital for months. We'd finally run a battery of tests on him. And like most folks, he was scared waiting for the results to come back from the lab. When Dr. Christopher got the results Nick sought Him out late one night. Dr. Christopher broke the news to him over a cup of coffee in the cafeteria.

Nick asked Him, "Look, I know You're a great surgeon. One of the best. If You weren't, You couldn't perform all these incredible miracles of Yours. You've got quite a following. So give it to me straight. I can take it."

And Dr. Christopher did. "You need major surgery, Nick."

Nick chuckled, "I lied. I can't take it."

Dr. Christopher went on, "I'm not talking about bypass. That won't do it. You need a new heart."

"I'm an old man, Doc. I can't start over."

"Yes you can, Nick."

"So, what are You saying . . . my life's in Your hands?"

"Always has been, Nick. You've just gotta trust Me. Believe Me, I wanna give you a ticker that'll never stop! But you've gotta make a leap of faith."

And that's the point He tried to make with all of us. I don't know what happened to Nick or how he's doing. I hope and pray he made that leap. You see, that's the place where so many of us stay . . . just on the edge of wonder, fearing the mystery. Never fully living, some of us with barely a pulse.

But those of us who jump the chasm never look back. Why, I've done things in His name that I never could've done in the name of the AMA! I even still make house calls. Those of us who studied directly under Dr. Christopher know He expects that of us.

I guess that's why I still make these visits. Health screenings, we call them nowadays. (Looks at the clipboard again) Looking at your chart, you seem pretty healthy. Looks like you're staying active, doing all the things you need to be doing.

(Takes out the stethoscope and places it in his ears) But let's give a listen to the heart and make sure we're fully alive. (Holds out the other end to the audience, listening for a heartbeat, blackout)

SIMON THE ZEALOT

NOTE: When Jesus is arrested, it is recorded in the Gospels that some-one drew a sword and struck one of the servants of the high priest. On-ly in the Book of John is this person given the identity of Simon Peter. The other Gospels refer to him as "one of Jesus' companions" or as "one of those standing near."

It is not uncommon to transfer certain events from lesser to more important figures in history. In fact, it is quite common and there is some precedent to suggest that this is perhaps what John has done.

Historically though, due to the violent and revolutionary nature of the Zealots there is some basis for Simon, the only Zealot among the Twelve, to be the one most ready and inclined to draw the sword. He is also the one most apt to be armed and carrying a weapon and to have the impulse to use it in such a situation. For those reasons, in the fol-lowing monologue I have chosen to put the sword in Simon the Zealot's hand.

PRODUCTION NOTE: Some of the vernacular may change as time passes. Feel free to update the slang as needed.

(AT RISE: Simon is dressed in street clothes, perhaps even a muscle shirt and some rather dirty jeans. He is in his mid-20s to early 30s. He has lived his life in oppression and poverty. His education has come from the streets. He is a black man.)

SIMON *(pacing about, delivered in a rhythmic voice à la Rev. Jesse Jackson):* Gather round peoples and hear my story! My name is ZeeMan and it's a story 'bout love and not hate, a story 'bout light in the middle of the dark, a story 'bout hope in the middle of despair! It ain't no fairy tale neither. It ain't about no Crips and no Bloods, but about the blood of a Savior! It ain't about drive-bys and needless death, but about an empty grave! *(Raises his fists in the air)* It ain't about a fist raised in violence *(slowly opens his fists and stretches his arms out like a cross),* but about a palm open to sacrifice!

You see, I been there. ZeeMan knows what it is to live without hope in the city. My grandaddy watched our hope try to ride the bus down in Selma, Ala. My momma seen our dream gunned down on a balcony in D.C. And I seen how far we come watching our brother get his rights beaten into him, right here in the city of Angels! The whole world seen that on video. But did it make any diff'rence come jury time? Unh-uh! Things is still black and white, and they ain't no shades of gray as far as I can see! So it ain't no wonder we smashed some glass and burned some city over that one. And I be the first to tell you I stood on the street corner and threw a few bricks too.

So when the Man comes up to me and says, "ZeeMan, put down the brick and pick up the cross," I'm thinkin' where'd this homey come from? It ain't from South Central, that's for sure. And how come He know my name? Only the brothers call me that. You see, Momma named me Simon but the gang called me ZeeMan due to my skill with a razor—kinda like Zorro, only I don't need no black mask.

I says to the Man, "Don't be trippin' on me. You put down your brick here and somebody else gonna pick it up and use it on your head!" He leans into me and gets right in my face and says, "You want change and so do I. I'm here to lead the revolution, but this ain't the way."

I says, "Man, what You talkin' 'bout revolution? Nothin' changes around here but the players. The score gonna always stay the same. We been *o*ppressed, *sup*pressed, and *de*pressed for so long I got no voice without this brick! The system ain't never changin' without this. (*Shakes imaginary brick*) The only change I can see is with this brick in my hand."

The Man says, "You got nothin' in your hand but trouble. I'm here to turn the system upside down. I'm here to show you how to love those that hate you, how to pray for those that beat you down."

I says, "We been beaten down since we first sucked air." The Man says, "Lay the brick down, ZeeMan. Ride the bus with Me for a few days and see what I mean."

So I get on the bus with the Man and His homeboys and we head on down the Santa Ana freeway and catch 405 headin' west. Now I knows where I belong and it ain't down there. I stick out there like a white boy does in the NBA! But the Man says we gonna check out one o' His daddy's houses. We get there and it's this big ol' building made entirely outta glass. It's the biggest mirror I ever seed! You look at yourself in the reflection just right and your ego is as tall as the building! Got this big ol' flashin' neon sign out front says "Jesus Christ Enterprises Unlimited."

Oowee, we's lucky to get in the door! It was like an air-conditioned city unto itself. They got ever'thin' you ever dreamed of and some stuff you ain't! They got a drive-in service where you don't even leave your car for the sermon; a drive-thru car wash and baptism where you choose sprinkle, spray, or dunk; a bowlin' alley, glow-in-the-dark praying hands, a Christmas pageant with real flyin' angels you could see on pay-per-view, even a little kneelin' Santa Claus you could have for your own Nativity set at home with a minimum donation. Everthin' was for sale, man . . . even the ferns. They made the Home Shoppin' Network look like a garage sale. They had the merchandisin' rights to the Man sewn up! And business was gooood . . .

Well, the Man goes insane on us! He starts runnin' through the aisles dumpin' over the bingo tables and upsettin' the expresso carts in the lobby and throwing the vendors through the glass. And He's screamin' at the top a' His lungs the whole time He's shatterin' all the mirrors, "You can't sell My love for profit! My house is for prayer, but you all turnin' it into some kind a' shoppin' mall! Get out! All of you!"

Well, I like what I see . . . now we're talking insurrection. The only thing missin' is a brick in His hand. So I told the Man, "Listen, You wanna do some real damage let's go down to city hall and throw some rocks. That's where the real power is! And You need more visibility. We go downtown and we bound to get some media coverage."

"You just don't get it, do you, ZeeMan? You don't know what real power is. Real power is bein' willin' to let 'em slap both your cheeks. Real power is knowin' how to lay down in order to be raised up."

(Mockingly) "Yeah?" I said. "Stop dissin' me and prove it!" (Beat, then) And four days later He did.

Thursday night we was sleepin' on the lawns up around Mullholland Drive in Beverly Hills. I knowed we didn't belong there either, but the Man didn't seem to belong anywhere. The black and whites show up and start doin' their thing on the Man. Maybe I seen too many of my brothers go down, but I wasn't lettin' the Man go down without a fight. I pulled out my blade and cut one of the heat across the face. But the Man stopped me before I hardly got started.

"ZeeMan, put the knife down. It ain't the way of My revolution. Don't you know by now? You draw the sword, you're gonna die by the sword. Make your choice, ZeeMan . . ."

"What kinda riot is this, Jesus? You just gonna lay down and die!"

And the Man gets right in my face again and says, "That's right. It's the way it is. Make your choice, ZeeMan . . ."

The hardest thing I ever done was to let that blade slide to the ground and watch the law take Him away. But I did. 'Cause that's what He wanted . . . and I loved the Man. And that love finally began to take over my anger, my hatred at the system. And I begun to grasp the Man's words.

You see, the Man wasn't talkin' 'bout a change in the system, in some guv'ment policy. He wasn't talkin' 'bout the poor man winnin' the lottery, He wasn't talkin' 'bout leadin' another Watts riot, He wasn't talkin' 'bout no revolution of the people.

He was talkin' 'bout a revolution of the heart, a riot at the core of my being, 'bout a change in direction, a shift in my soul. He said He'd beat death only by dyin'. That He'd be raised up by layin' down. And He did it! He proved His words. And I ain't seen no other brother do that: no gang leader, no preacher, no mayor, no Malcolm X, nobody! Nobody but the Man come back from bein' dead! And that ain't no fairy tale neither. 'Cause I'm tellin' ya straight up, I seen it!

So now I make my way all over the City of Angels—from the Hood to Santa Monica, from Venice Beach to Burbank! Talkin' 'bout the Man and the miracle! So gather round, peoples, and hear my story! A story 'bout love and not hate, a story 'bout light in the middle of the dark, a story 'bout hope in the middle of despair! It ain't about no Crips and no Bloods, but about the blood of a Savior! It ain't about drive-bys and needless death, but about an empty grave! *(Raises his fists in the air)* It ain't about a fist raised in violence *(slowly opens his fists and stretches his arms out),* but about a palm open to sacrifice . . . *(Blackout)*

JUDAS

NOTE: Judas Iscariot has come to be the symbol of betrayal and treachery. And it seems only his due course to have died an ignoble death for his disloyalty.

However, the disposition and nature of Judas can be found in all of us. What have men not betrayed throughout history? Their country, their leaders, their loved ones, even their faith. And are there not people around us who continue to sell out for less than what God calls them to be? Who among us hasn't at one time or another sold off a piece of our soul? Whether it be in the workplace, in our homes, with our friends, even in our church. Judas Iscariot is a vivid reminder that, but for the grace of God, we are all guilty.

To this author's way of thinking, Judas' greatest sin was not betraying Jesus. We've all done that at one time in our lives to one degree or another. Judas' great weakness was in not recognizing the mercy and grace of a Savior who hung on a cross with His arms spread wide to embrace and forgive all humanity. And what separates us from Judas is whether we choose to step into that embrace or run from it into the dark.

AT RISE: Judas is seated at a table with a pile of quarters and a magnifying glass on it. He looks very nondescript, dressed casually in contemporary clothing, nothing about his manner would draw attention to him. He looks just like you and me.)

JUDAS *(he is just finishing stacking the quarters in little piles of fours before him):* "Twenty-eight . . . twenty-nine . . . thirty." *(Glancing at audience, continuing to rearrange his coins)* I've always been fascinated by coins. When I was a little boy my dad gave me a coin collection for my birthday. I used to spend hours staring at nickels and dimes and pennies under a magnifying glass, looking for the flaws that would make them worth more than just their face value.

Jesus was the same way, I guess. He gathered the 12 of us around Him to start His church. And we all had flaws, but He saw hidden value in each of us. Look at Peter and John. Even Matt and Tom had a purpose. *(Skeptically)* Go figure that one out.

Me? *(Holds the magnifying glass up to one eye)* I was put in charge of finances. Not a good idea, as it turned out. *(Rubbing his thumb and fingers together)* Sticky fingers, I guess. My name is . . . *(hesitates, lowers the magnifying glass to the table)* No, my name isn't important. Most of you know it, anyway. If you hear my name, you might not listen to what I want to tell you. And I want you to hear it. I think it's important.

(Stands and crosses to the front of the table) When Mary brought that pint of Oil of Olay out, I thought maybe she was gonna donate it to our movement. It was pretty valuable stuff. I'd priced it before at the duty-free shops. But when she began rubbing it on Jesus' feet, I couldn't sit still!

I said to Him *(indignantly)*, "Why waste all that oil on Your feet? We all know it's not gonna actually take any years off Your life. We should've sold it and used the proceeds to feed and clothe the homeless and the indigent. They're a bit more important than Your wrinkled toes!"

Boy, that sounded good rolling off my tongue. I clothed my intent in piety. And it came so easily! I thought that maybe Jesus had missed my true calling. I shouldn't be church treasurer, I should be executive pastor! But He knew my heart wasn't in it. He knew where my heart was and where my treasure lay.

(Picks up a quarter and holds it out admiringly before him, examining it closely) I mean, have you ever really *felt* a quarter before? I hated it when they started putting copper in the middle. It took away from the weight of pocket change. Silver is so much better. It's so much smoother to the touch. *(With slight regret)* Even if your hand's too callused to feel.

(Chummy, justifying) Listen, you know how it is . . . it starts with a box of paper clips from the office, a couple of envelopes out of the supply room. You start writing off personal lunches as business meetings. And it just gets easier after that. Nothing unusual about me having my hand in the till too. *(Casually)* After all, it's in our nature, isn't it?

(Beat, then) But that's where I kept getting hung up. He'd come to change our nature. *(Frustrated with himself)* And I knew it up here *(tapping his head)*, I just didn't know it here *(taps his chest)*. I don't know how I missed it. I heard His words, saw His miracles, and still . . . I missed the boat.

I missed His last meal too. John said He preached one of His best sermons at that Last Supper. But I had to leave the party early, took my wine and bread on the run while the others lingered. *(Honestly)* The sacraments went down easily. Nothing got stuck in my throat. *(Offhandedly)* I'm experiencing a bit of an aftertaste now, though. I guess that's to be expected when you drink to someone else's end.

Some people say I sold Him out. But I don't think so. He sold himself out. He knew where He was heading. And I just saw the handwriting on the wall, as they say. *(Ominous)* The crowds were growing restless, and you could feel the tension hanging in the air. The buzzards were circling overhead. Something had to give. And I saw no reason that I should come up empty-handed. Like any prudent person I planned ahead.

When it came time I could've just pointed Him out to them. I didn't have to embrace Him. Funny thing about a hug. You can't look over your own shoulder and do it. For the moment it takes, you've got to trust the other person. *(Shaking his head sadly)* He should've known that . . .

(Holding his arms out, as if embracing someone, reliving it slowly) Yet, as I held my arms out . . . I stopped. And for the briefest of moments, I hesitated at what I was about to do. *(Shocked)* And it was in that moment that He! . . . *He* stepped into *my* arms! And as I closed my hands around Him . . . I knew that in that moment He was embracing all of us. Not just me, a traitor. *(Struggling to get the words out)* But He was embracing the whole human race—all of His betrayers, all of us who would be deceitful, who would break faith with Him, who would pledge our loyalty and then break His heart . . . from the beginning of time until the end.

That's why He had come. *(Desperately)* And I knew it up here! *(Taps head again)* . . . But not where it mattered. *(Drops hand to his heart)* For, you see, we all betrayed Him. Even the best of us denied Him and ran into the night. *(Crosses back behind the table and sits)*

But that's where the similarity ends. Come morning, Peter found his way back to Jesus. Whereas, I continue to sit in the dark and rub coins together.

My greatest sin was not my betrayal. No, for we have all turned traitor and run from Him at one time or another. *(Achingly)* My greatest sin is not finding my way back to Him. I cannot see beyond these coins to a Savior full of love, mercy, and forgiveness.

(Picks up a stack of coins and rearranges them, lights slowly begin to dim) Instead, I sit here and try to rearrange my shattered conscience. . . . Trying to sort out the price of one soul. *(Staring at the table, stands)* Thirty dollars doesn't get you much nowadays. Down payment on a burial plot, perhaps 10 feet of good stout rope. *(Looks up, haunted)* O God, I am forever in the dark.

(Searching the audience, reaching out) But you . . . you are on the edge of light. But I am your shadow. You do well to not forget me. For my name . . . is the same as yours. And should we bump into each other in the dark, remember me. *(Blackout)*